Pieced Hexies

A New Tradition in English Paper Piecing

By Mickey Depre

Pieced Hexies
A New Tradition in English Paper Piecing

By Mickey Depre

Editor: Deb Rowden
Designer: Kelly Ludwig
Photography: Aaron T. Leimkuehler
Illustration: Eric Sears
Technical Editor: Kathe Dougherty
Production assistance: Jo Ann Groves

Published by:
Kansas City Star Books
1729 Grand Blvd.
Kansas City, Missouri, USA 64108

First edition, third printing
ISBN: 978-1-61169-062-0

Library of Congress Control Number: 2012943454

Printed in the United States of America by Walsworth Publishing Co., Marceline, MO

To order copies, call StarInfo at (816) 234-4636 and say "Books."

The Quilter's Home Page

www.PickleDish.com

Contents

Hexie Designs

Acknowledgements

Never ever give up. That is my motto in life. It has served me well.

This book is truly more than just the pages it is written on, it is a passion for me. The idea of Pieced Hexies came to me in a time of my life when it was most needed. And creating these designs and imagining the places they could be used was truly a gift I wish to share.

The person who made this possible is my dear husband Paul. He is my rock. And I am the roll. Together, we never ever give up and dance away. And my children, Paul Jr. and Emily, who by just being give me something to smile about each and every day.

And finally all my friends, quilting and nonquilting, far and near, thank you for everything you bring to my life. You can never have too many friends in life. And I am lucky my path has crossed all of yours.

A special thanks to Doug Weaver and Diane McLendon for making this whirlwind happen. And to Edie McGinnis, you have no idea how much your words meant to me that you spoke at Market. Thank you.

And to my team at The Kansas City Star who jumped on this speeding train and took the ride: Eric Sears, Kelly Ludwig, Aaron Leimkuehler, Jo Ann Groves, and Kathe Dougherty. Thank you.

And finally to my editor Deb Rowden ... thank you for everything. I bet you are still wondering what hit you.

About the Author

Mickey Depre was introduced to the world of Fiber Arts by her own personal "grand masters" at the age of four. Grandmothers, great aunts, aunts and her mother filled her days with cloth, needles, yarn and such.

Textiles have always fascinated her from vintage to current and her taste has always been ALL! sewing in general, mending to garment making were never a chore.

In 1997 she found quilting on her own. She is the first quiltmaker in her family, but vows not to be the only one.

Chicago has been her lifelong home. Married to her high school sweetheart Paul, they are the proud parents of a set of grown twins, Paul Jr. and Emily. And then there is Molly, their miniature dachshund who now fills the "nest" with joy.

Mickey has quietly instilled her love of sewing into all their lives: husband, son and daughter - all can sew (it's a bit rough for Molly to reach the pedal so she is working on ironing skills). She is now waiting for one of them to want to share her stash.

Mickey enjoys sharing her love of fiber through lectures and workshops. Her workshops mix technique instruction with individual creativity and always a giggle or two. You can find more at her website www.mdquilts.com.

Whist Jubliance, 81" x 101". Stitched and quilted by Mickey Depre, 2012. I named this quilt for what it is to me "Quiet Joy." This is "that quilt" (quilters know what I am referring to) I daydream about a future great, great grandchild snuggling under. This quilt is a time stamp of my life.

Introduction

Cnglish Paper Piecing has been around for a long time. It came to America with the settlers. Imagine women in the colonial times making sure to utilize every scrap of fabric by basting it to paper shapes. These fabric covered paper shapes could then be sewn together, one by one, and over time they would create an entire quilt. Pioneer women far away from readily accessible fabric also used it to preserve every scrap. And with the resurgence of English Paper Piecing, especially in the form of the hexagon in the 1930s, even the tiniest bit of fabric was used to create quilts when economics may not have allowed the luxury of purchasing yardage.

I am a quilter with the good fortune to be known for my whimsical art quilts. But I also make traditional quilts. Some say the two do not mix. But I have been doing both behind the scenes for so many years that I hope to prove them wrong. If you look closely, you will see my nod to traditional piecing in my art quilts. And I still wield a needle for some hand appliqué. Now I hope to explain this in reverse at lectures. I am a traditional quilter who loves to express herself in the form of Art Quilts too.

My dance with English Paper Piecing began on October 18, 2011. The idea for Pieced Hexies was born just a few minutes later. My life has not been the same since.

But let's back up a bit for the whole story.

As a National Quilt Instructor, I spend a great portion of my life on the road, and thus in airports and hotel rooms across America. Since my laptop travels with me, I use my downtime to try to accomplish all the business end of being a traveling teacher so I can take full advantage of studio time when I am home.

I like the keep creativity in my life so there is always a little project stashed away in the precious square foot of personal space in my suitcase. For years this space held yarn and knitting needles. Then a dear friend showed me her Hexie quilt - 13 years in the making. I took one look at that quilt and ordered my first pack of die cut papers as soon as I was home. Her quilt is composed of ¾" Hexies. Her 13 years of on and off work rang in my head. I elected to order 1 ½" Hexies to hopefully shave some time off the project life.

The papers arrived and promptly sat in my studio for 9 months.

When I was packing for an engagement and looking for something new to do on the road, I quickly grabbed the papers and some 3 ½" scrap squares and tossed them into my suitcase.

On the second night in the hotel I pulled them out. I basted 7 Hexies and as I was sewing them together into a rosette I started to think ... what if? Designs danced in my head.

I dropped the handwork and began sketching furiously. I couldn't draw the Hexies and write notes fast enough. I didn't have a sewing machine with me but I had scotch tape (why to this day I don't know ... a bit surreal) and I literally taped my first pieced Hexie together. Oh my, I was excited. I snapped a picture and sent it off to two people, that friend who introduced me to English Paper Piecing and my dear husband Paul. Both responded immediately. Their response told me I was on to something.

I pretty much stayed up all night drawing and taping. I caught my flight home in the morning and was in the studio sewing my first Pieced Hexie within hours.

This book contains the "Original 7" as I call them. They are first 7 designs that I drew that night. These seven evolve into 63 designs found on these pages. But this is just the beginning. As noted in the Sparkle design, if you inadvertently reverse some piecing, you have a new design. Or what if you combine some designs as shown throughout the book?

The possibilities are endless!

There are no patterns in this book. It is meant to give you instruction to make these blocks (yes I think of the rosettes as blocks) that you can in turn apply to any Hexie pattern on the market or in your imagination.

The Hexie segments by no means must end up in the traditional rosette. Try just putting three together in what I call a "Hexie Smile." Or a row of the pieced Hexies side by side in a long length.

And finally, there is no rule that your entire Hexie project must be composed of just Hexies. They are wonderful accents to all kinds of creative adventures ... and this will totally help you dodge that 13 year timetable.

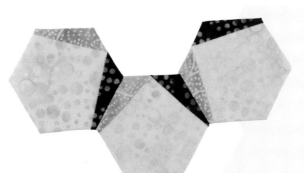

For those of you who love Electric Quilt as much as I do, be sure to check my resource guide (page 95). There is some information there for further design ideas.

So let's begin ... and don't blame me ... they are addicting ... you have been forewarned.

Hex On!

Mickey

P.S. Many thanks to Bonnie K. Hunter and her "Lady in Waiting" Hexie Quilt Project. You are truly a friend who has changed my life.

General Supplies

Just the FAQs ma'am.

What exactly is a Hexie?

A Hexie is the nickname that has been given to any size English Paper Piecing Hexagon shape. You can buy these papers in die cut packs at your local quilt shop or you can print them out using your computer and heavyweight paper at home. If you cut them out yourself, take your time and be precise so your Hexies finish at the proper size. There are several websites that have Hexie pdfs/jpegs that you can download for printing (page 95).

What size Hexie do I need to make the patterns in this book?

All the patterns in this book are made using a 1 ½" Hexie (see templates on pages 33, 57, and 65). Hexies are referred to by the length of one edge of the shape. Thus every edge is 1 ½" on a 1 ½" Hexie. The center measurement or width of any Hexie is twice the edge length. So a 1 ½" Hexie is 3" wide. But note a Hexie is not as tall as it is wide. Due to the nature of the shape they are a bit on the short side. So a 1 ½" Hexie is only 2 ⅝" tall.

What size piece of fabric do I need to cover my Hexie?

All the patterns in this book are made using a 3 ½" pieced square and basting it to a Hexie. There is a little bit of waste but it is easier to piece a 3 ½" square than a 3 ½" x 3 ⅛" rectangle. Sometimes a little waste is ok.

Based on this I also cut 3 ½" squares for use in the centers of my Pieced Hexie Rosettes.

Do I need a special needle?

Actually I recommend two.

I like John James self threading needle for basting. This needle has a little lever on top so all you have to do is hold your basting thread over it, tug down, and voila! Your needle and thread are ready to go.

To sew Hexies together, I like a fine milliner's needle. A pack of Richard Hemming & Son Milliners size 11 can always be found in my sewing box. The size is up to you. Try starting off with a larger needle for ease if you are new to handwork. Once you feel comfortable, scale down to a finer needle for more delicate stitches.

What happens if I have difficulty threading my hand needle?

I highly recommend the purchase of a needle threader. I would be lost without my Clover table top threader in my arsenal of tools.

And thread - what about thread?

Here is a sticky wicket. Experiment! My current favorites are below but I am always trying new threads and have found that sometimes there are certain threads for certain types of cotton. And of course different threads - just like needles - for different jobs.

For basting, use leftover spools of thread. See you have now found a project that you can use that half spool of blaring orange leftover from your pumpkin costume. Remember basting thread is just temporary so any color goes.

To sew Hexies together, I go back and forth between a fine silk thread (YLI brand) doubled for strength and a 60 weight cotton thread (Presencia). I find that both give me the ability to have hidden stitches as they sink nicely into the fabrics. I use silk particularly when working with batiks and hand dyed fabrics. They usually have a tight weave due to being prewashed. So now you have figured out I don't prewash my cottons ... that is a whole other obsession and I don't care to go there.

How about some protection for my fingertip?

I use a thimble, a leather coin thimble to be exact. Experiment here too and find what feels most comfortable for you. Remember that some thimbles (i.e. leather ones) take a bit of time and use to wear in and fit properly so don't discard a thimble choice too soon.

Pins? Can one ever have enough pins?

I use a fine long shafted pin for my Hexies. 'Nuff said.

Can I run with my scissors?

No, I never condone running with scissors. Miss Schrage, my kindergarten teacher, drilled that into my head. But I do love a good pair of scissors. For this project, you might want to have two different blades close by: a pair of fabric cutting scissors for trimming down your 3 ½" square when you are basting and a pair of small embroidery scissors that can easily tuck into your "on the go box/bag" for use. Hexies are wonderful on-the-go projects and great conversation starters at ball games, doctor offices, school functions (oh how I wish I was making Hexies when I attended years of band performances ... the projects I could have had completed ...).

Why piece a rosette?

My Hexie journey started with the traditional rosette because that was what I saw in patterns everywhere. Most of the samples in the book are done in the rosette style. But that is just the tip of the design field for Pieced Hexies. I see chevron quilts, and border treatments, and a multitude of other applications ... let your imagination run wild.

What's an "On the Go" box/bag?

Simple. A collection of all the items necessary to baste or sew together a few Hexies in those snippets of time we all have in our daily lives when you can. Besides the examples stated above ... on the train, lunch break, coffee break, and especially at night when you are watching TV or listening to some music. Hexies are great friends too as your hands are busy with them and not reaching for the chip bowl. Just sayin'.

Do you ever have to "unsew"?

Yes it happens all the time. Unsewing is basically what you will do when you are removing the basting from your Hexie after all six sides have been stabilized or connected to another hexagon. For this you need a good sharp seam ripper. Check my resource guide (page 95) for the information regarding beautiful hand-turned handled seam rippers. It is very nice to have at least one of these to call your own.

English Paper Piecing Instructions

Basic Basting

1. Place your selected fabric on the table in front of you with the wrong side facing up.

2. Pin your paper to the fabric allowing at least ¼" around all edges.

3. Trim fabric leaving a ¼" seam using your paper for guidance regarding the shape.

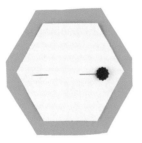

4. Fold the excess fabric over the paper piece and baste using a large running stitch around all the edges. Fold the corner inward like a mitered binding . and make sure your basting stitches run over each corner to hold the folded fabric flat and stable.

The Sewing Together

1. Hold 2 Hexies together right sides touching and edges lined up.

2. Knot the end of your sewing thread. Run your needle about ½" from the corner of your edge. This will place your knot away from the corner and will reduce the bulk that tends to build up in this area.

3. Take two stitches in the corner to secure it. You want your small whip stitches to just catch the edges of the fabric. Try not to sew thru the paper. You may nick it a few times when you first start out. Don't worry, it's ok.

4. Now here is where I do things a little bit different. After the initial first couple of whip stitches I open up the Hexies so that they lay flat in my hand and continue to sew. I gently run the needle thru the fabric and across the paper. Think buttonhole stitch without the carrying of the thread across. This gives me no exposure of my stitches on the front of the Hexies for a crisp clean appearance.

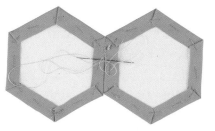

5. When I reach the opposite corner, I either continue sewing adding another Hexie on (make sure to really secure those corners by double stitching at the end of one side and at the beginning of another) or later you may find small openings/holes at the joining corners of your hexies.

6. When you either run out of thread or Hexies, it's time to knot off. Run your needle back towards the center of an edge length again (as you did to start) and then knot off. Again keep your corners as bulk free as possible.

7. When all sides of a Hexie have been stabilized/sewn to another, remove the basting threads and the paper Hexie from the back. The paper piece can be used again.

Pieced Hexie Basting Instructions

Now that you've learned about English Paper Piecing, let's tailor that style to Pieced Hexie paper piecing.

It is my preference to use needle and thread for basting Hexies. It just seems to keep the seams from shifting out of alignment. By stitching over the folded corners keeps them as flat as can be. You can use a gluestick for basting if you prefer. The choice is yours but give the following method a try, at least once. Sometimes "old school" is best.

A Tumbler block (page 46) is shown in these pictures. Remember, these instructions can be applied to any of the designs in the book.

It is very important to trim your seam allowances to a scant ⅛" immediately after sewing every seam. With this is mind, I suggest you lower your stitch number to slightly lower than your default for a tighter stitch. If you forget to trim as you sew, don't worry ... just trim before basting.

⊛ Pieced Hexie designs are based on each paper hexagon being covered with a simple pieced 3 ½" square.

⊛ Turn the pieced block so the wrong side is facing you.

⊛ You must use a 1 ½" size hexagon for this method. This measurement pertains to the length of each side. The center width measurement of this hexagon is 3". The height measurement is 2 ⅝".

⊛ Following the individual instructions given in each pattern section, you will draw alignment guidelines on your hexagon.

⊛ Place the paper hexagon with drawn guidelines on top of the pieced 3 ½" square. Line up the drawn guidelines with the **seam** lines.

Pin the paper hexagon in place. Use a pin with a longer shaft and put at least ¾" to 1" of space between pin holes to keep the hexagon as flat as possible.

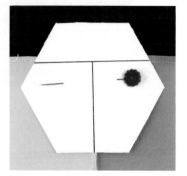

Trim excess fabric away leaving a generous ¼" around the hexagon. Note that at the center points the seam allowance might be slightly smaller.

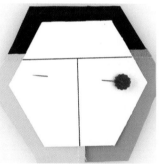

Begin your running basting stitch on an edge that contains a seam so you can secure it immediately. Tuck in excess material on the corners like you would if miter binding on a quilt or making a bed. Be sure to make a stitch over the turn fold created as you move from one side of the hexagon to the other.

This hexagon lays as flat as can be with all the corner folds held down with a running stitch over them. On the final fold, make 2 running stitches over the fold in the shape of a "plus" sign, draw the thread one last half stitch to the back and simply clip. No need to knot at the end ... the double stitching will hold the basting stitch in place.

This is your basted Pieced Hexie from the front. Only 5 more to go to make a Hexie rosette!

Spike

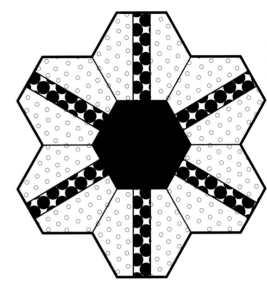

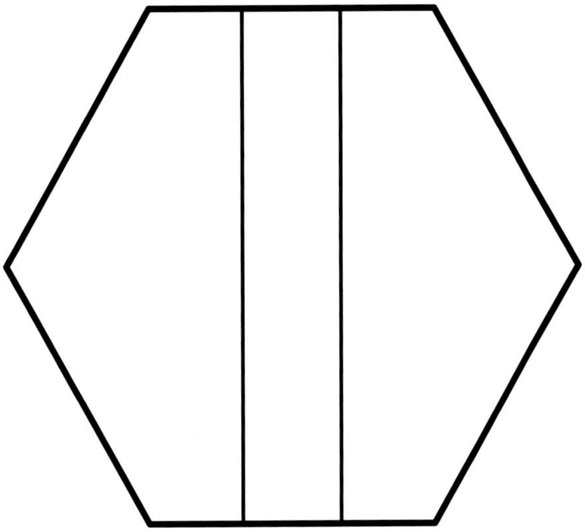

Be sure to read about *General Supplies, English Paper Piecing Instructions, and Pieced Hexie Basting Instructions* before you start.

These instructions are for piecing 6 – 3 ½" squares for each Spike rosette. The center hexagon is a solid fabric – no piecing instructions are needed, just use a 3 ½" square.

Important - Trim pieced seams to ⅛" after each one is sewn. This will reduce bulk for basting!

Material Needed for 1 Square

- �֍ Fabric A: (2) 1 ¾" x 3 ½"
- ✖ Fabric B: (1) 1" x 3 ½"

Fabric Preparation

- ✖ Sew A to each lengthwise edge of B.

— OR —

Material Needed for 6 Squares

- ✖ Fabric A: (2) 1 ¾" x 22"
- ✖ Fabric B: (1) 1" x 22"

Fabric Preparation

- ✖ Sew the strips together lengthwise in an A-B-A pattern. Press the seam toward fabric A.

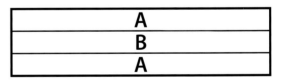

- ✖ Cut the A-B-A strip into 3 ½" segments to make finished 3 ½" squares.

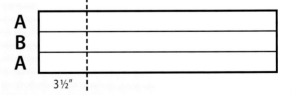

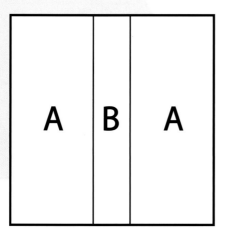

3 ½" Spike sewn square

Paper Preparation

Now baste the sewn square to the paper pattern. Perfect alignment is important, mark your paper hexagon with the alignment guides shown. Use a sharp pointed pencil or fine tip pen to mark lines. To mark accurately, angle your marking instrument tip into the groove of the ruler and paper.

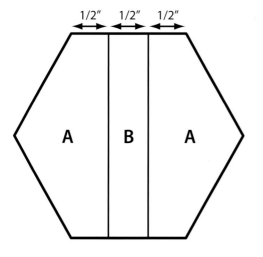

Spike Alignment Guides

⊛ Draw 2 guidelines from one hexagon edge vertically to the direct opposite edge.

⊛ Space the lines ½" from each corner/ hexagon edge and ½" apart from each other.

Assembly

⊛ Place the sewn square with the seam side facing up.

⊛ Place the marked paper pattern on top of the sewn square with markings facing up.

⊛ Line up the sewn seams and paper marks. Carefully pin once in the center, securing the sewn square to the paper.

⊛ Trim away excess fabric, leaving a generous ¼" on each side for basting.

⊛ Baste the sewn square to the paper hexagon, using a running stitch. *Start your basting on an edge with a seam to secure.*

⊛ ***Do not*** *remove the pin until at least 3 sides are basted.*

Spike Original A

Mic's Musings: Spike Hexie is the first Pieced Hexie I designed. It was quickly joined by many more images, but Spike will always be extra special to me.

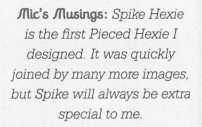

⊛ Make sure to have a great deal of contrast in color, shade, and/or print.

Spike Original B

⊗ Use a new fabric for all the right hand side A's.

Mic's Musings: When using a stripe in a very narrow part of a design ... think outside the box and have it run horizontally. By doing so, the repetition of the stripe makes the design vibrate.

Spike Variation 1A

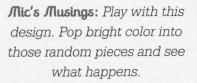

Mic's Musings: *Play with this design. Pop bright color into those random pieces and see what happens.*

- ⊛ Randomly piece fabric strip B using 2 high contrast fabrics.

- ⊛ **Note:** Iron the B seam created in this variation **open – do not** trim it down.

Spike Variation 1B

⊗ Try randomly piecing B using the same fabric as the center and a very high contrasting second fabric. Place the same fabric as center towards the center (touching) when assembling the rosette.

⊗ **Note:** Iron the B seam created in this variation **open** - **do not** trim it down.

Mic's Musings: This coloring gives the appearance that the center fabric is "spiking" out.

Cogs

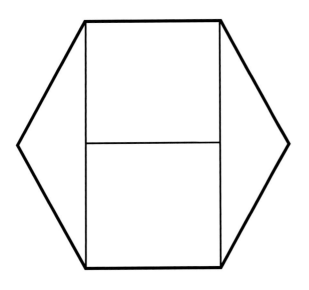

Be sure to read about *General Supplies, English Paper Piecing Instructions, and Pieced Hexie Basting Instructions* before you start.

These instructions are for piecing 6 – 3 ½" squares for each Cogs rosette.

The center hexagon is a solid fabric – no piecing instructions are needed, just use a 3 ½" square.

Important - Trim pieced seams to ⅛" after each one is sewn. This will reduce bulk for basting!

Material Needed for 1 Square

- Fabric A & B: 2" square
- Fabric C (2): 1 ¼" x 3 ½"

Fabric Preparation

- Sew A to B.
- Sew C lengthwise on each side of A/B unit.

— OR —

Material Needed for 6 Squares

- Fabric A & B: 2" x 13"
- Fabric C: (12) 1 ¼" x 3 ½"

Fabric Preparation

- Sew strips together lengthwise in A-B pattern.

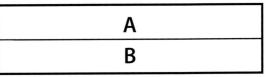

- Cut A-B into 2" segments and sew C lengthwise to each side of A/B unit.

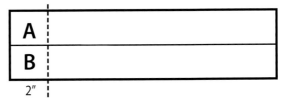

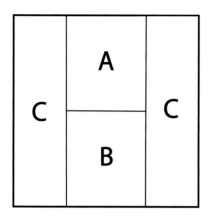

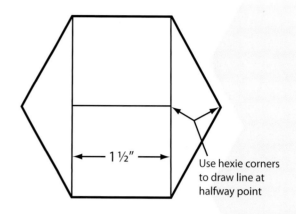

Use hexie corners to draw line at halfway point

1½"

3 ½" Cogs sewn square

Paper Preparation

Now baste the sewn square to the paper pattern. Perfect alignment is important, mark your paper hexagon with the alignment guides shown. Use a sharp pointed pencil or fine tip pen to mark lines. To mark accurately, angle your marking instrument tip into the groove of the ruler and paper.

Cogs Alignment Guides

- ✹ Place Hexie in front of you with a flat edge on top and bottom (as shown).
- ✹ Draw a vertical line from top left corner to bottom left corner. Repeat for the right side corners.
- ✹ Draw a horizontal line using the center corners as guides - connect the previously drawn lines.

Assembly

- ✹ Place the sewn square with the seam side facing up.
- ✹ Place the marked paper pattern on top of the sewn square with markings facing up.
- ✹ Line up the sewn seams and paper marks. Carefully pin once in the center, securing the sewn square to the paper.
- ✹ Trim away excess fabric, leaving a generous ¼" on each side for basting.
- ✹ Baste the sewn square to the paper hexagon, using a running stitch. *Start your basting on an edge with a seam to secure.*
- ✹ **Do not** remove the pin until at least 3 sides are basted.

Cogs Original A

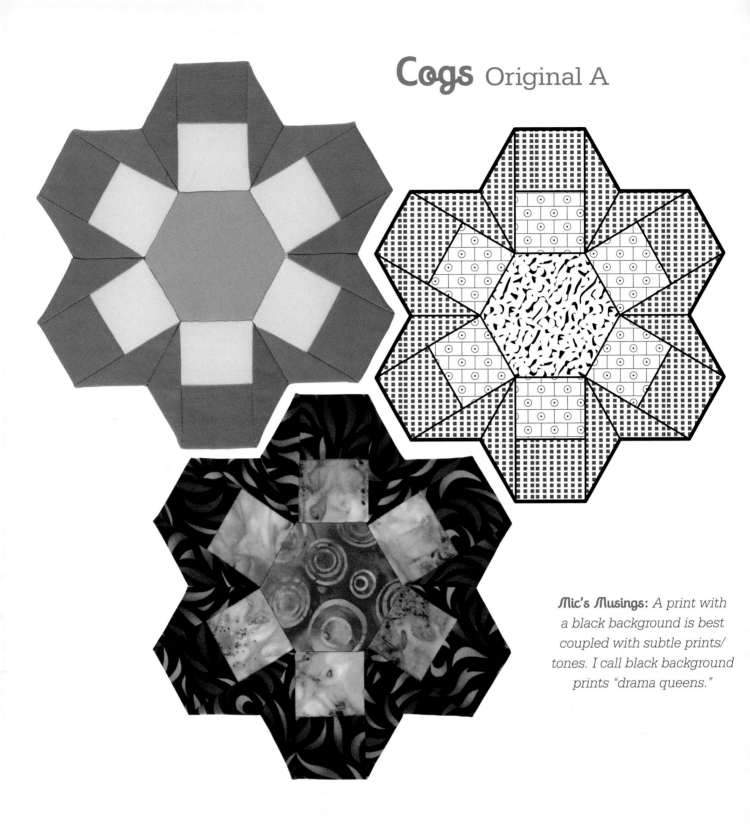

Mic's Musings: *A print with a black background is best coupled with subtle prints/ tones. I call black background prints "drama queens."*

Cogs Original B

✪ Change the color of the second square by using different C fabric.

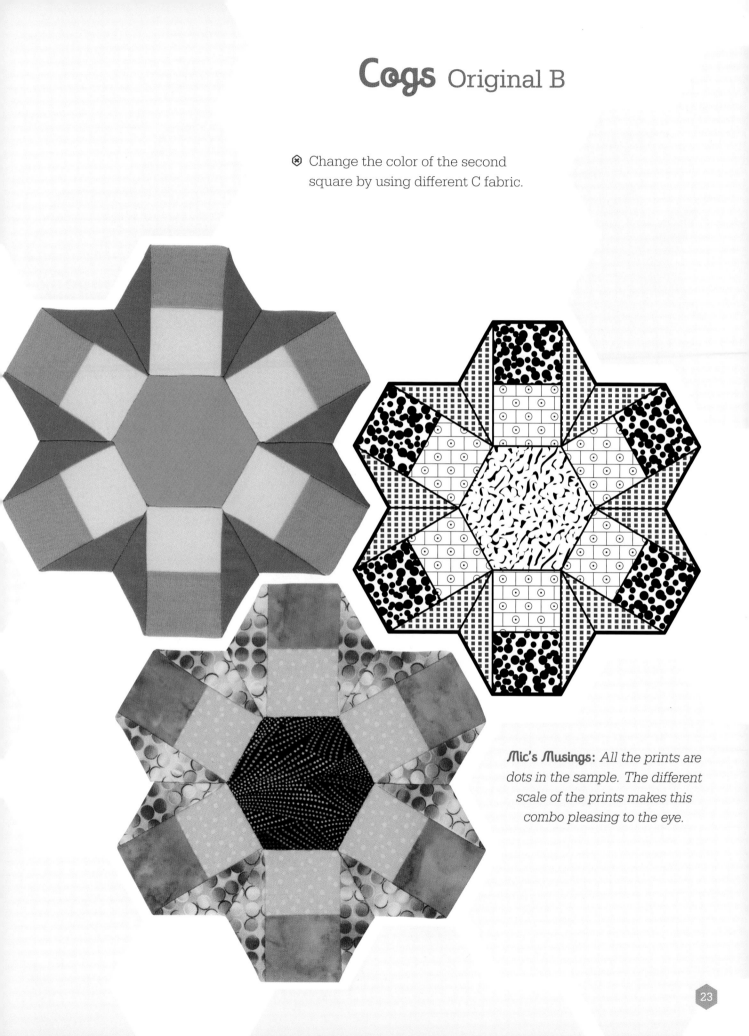

Mic's Musings: *All the prints are dots in the sample. The different scale of the prints makes this combo pleasing to the eye.*

Cogs Variation 1

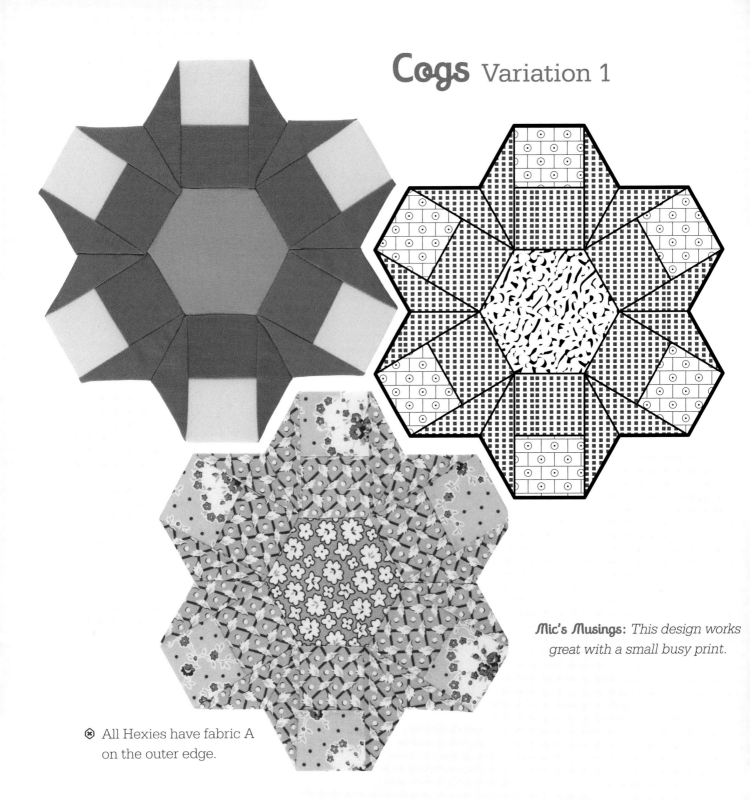

Mic's Musings: *This design works great with a small busy print.*

⊛ All Hexies have fabric A on the outer edge.

Cogs Variation 2A

✪ Twist each Hexie one turn clockwise.

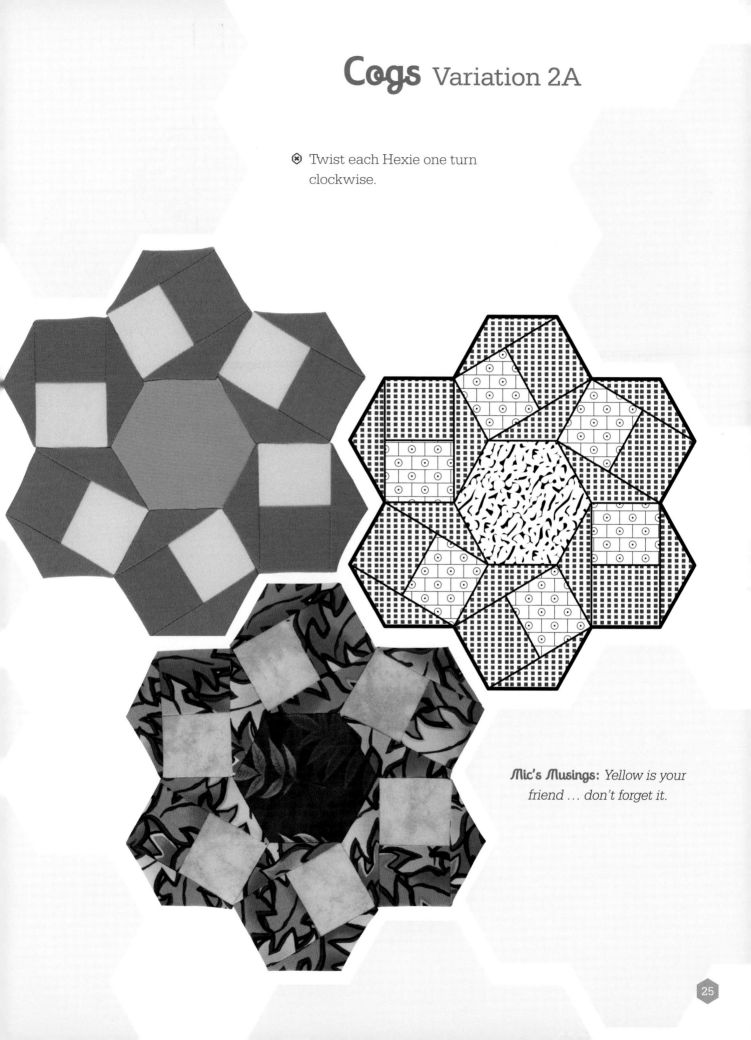

Mic's Musings: Yellow is your friend ... don't forget it.

Cogs Variation 2B

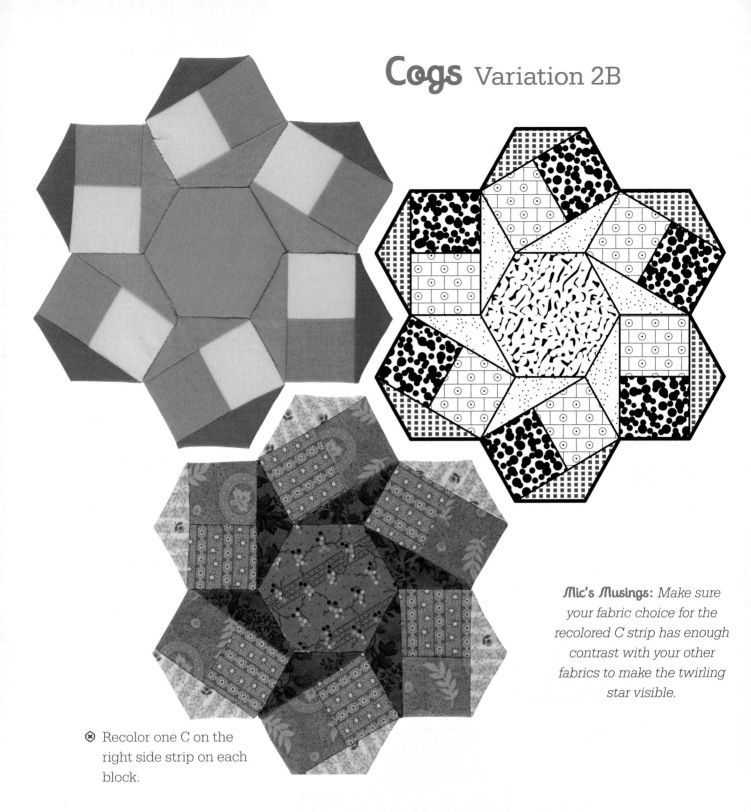

Mic's Musings: Make sure your fabric choice for the recolored C strip has enough contrast with your other fabrics to make the twirling star visible.

✪ Recolor one C on the right side strip on each block.

Cogs Variation 3A

- The top 3 Hexies have fabric A at the lower edge.

- The bottom 3 Hexies have fabric A at the upper edge.

Mic's Musings: Very busy can be very pleasing.

Cogs Variation 3B

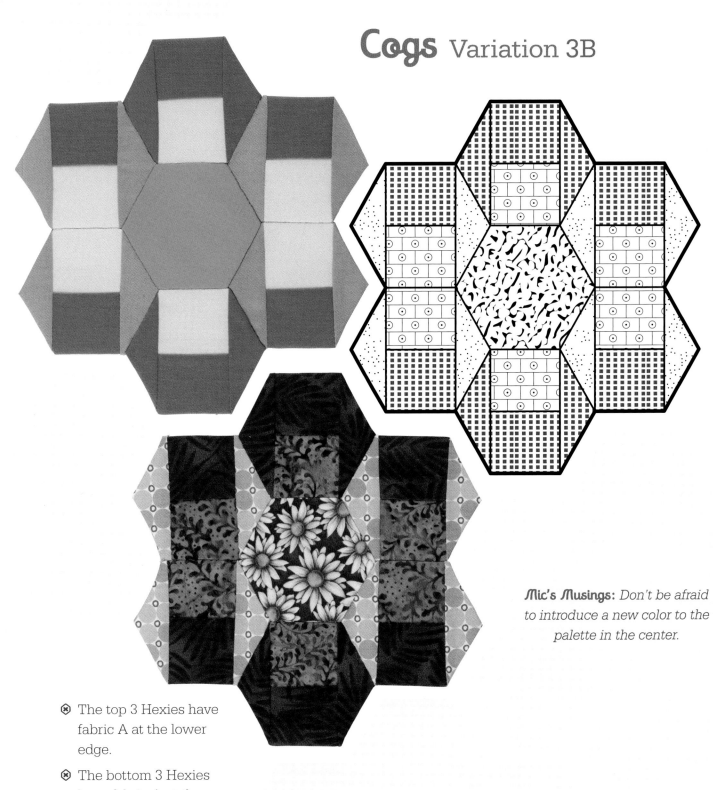

Mic's Musings: Don't be afraid to introduce a new color to the palette in the center.

- ⬡ The top 3 Hexies have fabric A at the lower edge.

- ⬡ The bottom 3 Hexies have fabric A at the upper edge.

- ⬡ Recolor the C strips on 4 Hexies.

Cogs Variation 4A

✴ Turn the outer Hexies towards the vertical center so fabric A does not touch an outer edge.

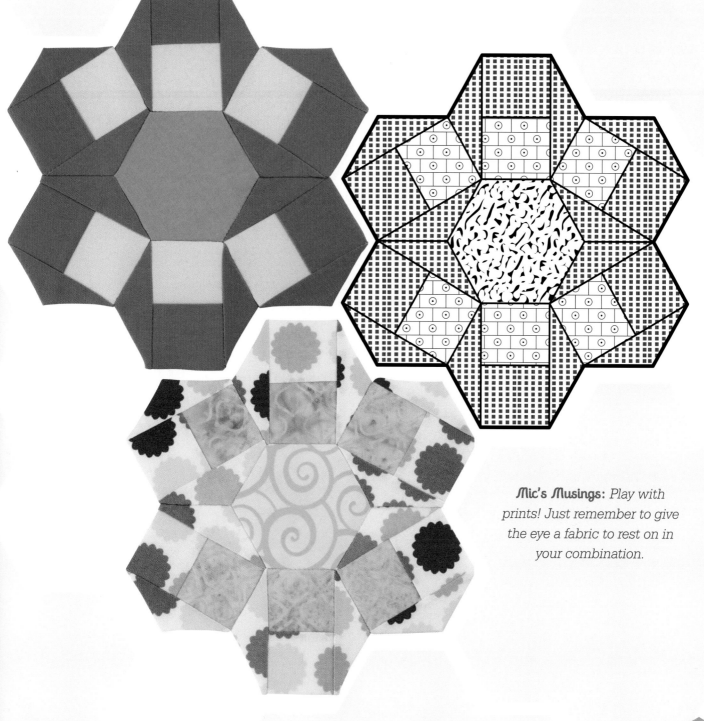

Mic's Musings: Play with prints! Just remember to give the eye a fabric to rest on in your combination.

Cogs Variation 4B

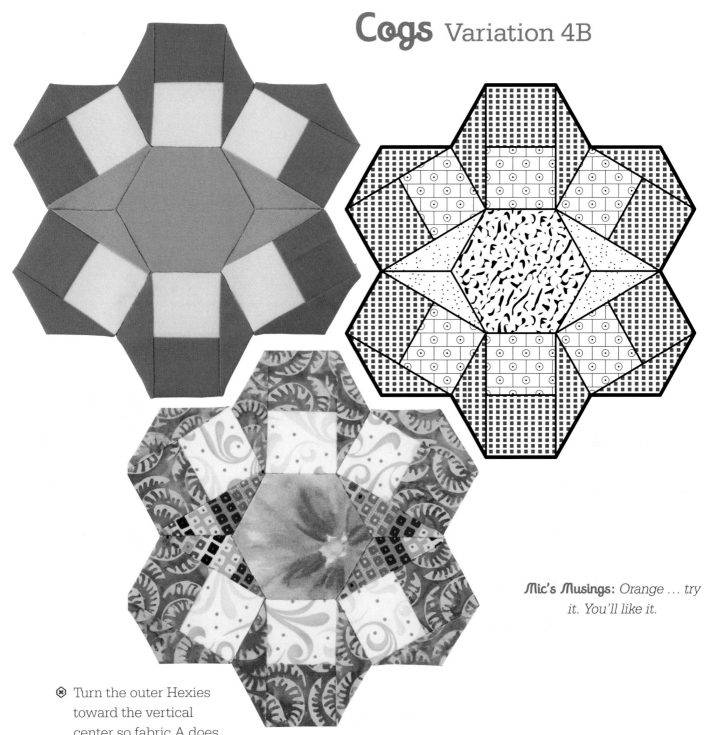

Mic's Musings: *Orange … try it. You'll like it.*

⬡ Turn the outer Hexies toward the vertical center so fabric A does not touch an outer edge.

⬡ Recolor the C strips of the turned Hexies that meet in the center. Two will be the left strip and 2 will be the right.

Cogs Variation 5A

⊛ Turn the outer Hexies toward the
outside edge with a lean to the
center of the design. Fabric A will
touch the outer edge.

*Mic's Musings: Black in the
center will guarantee the eye
goes there first.*

Cogs Variation 5B

 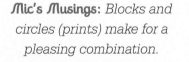

- ❋ Turn the outer Hexies toward the outside edge with a lean to the center of the design. Fabric A will touch the outer edge.

- ❋ Recolor the C strips of the turned Hexies that meet in the center. Two will be the left strip and 2 will be the right.

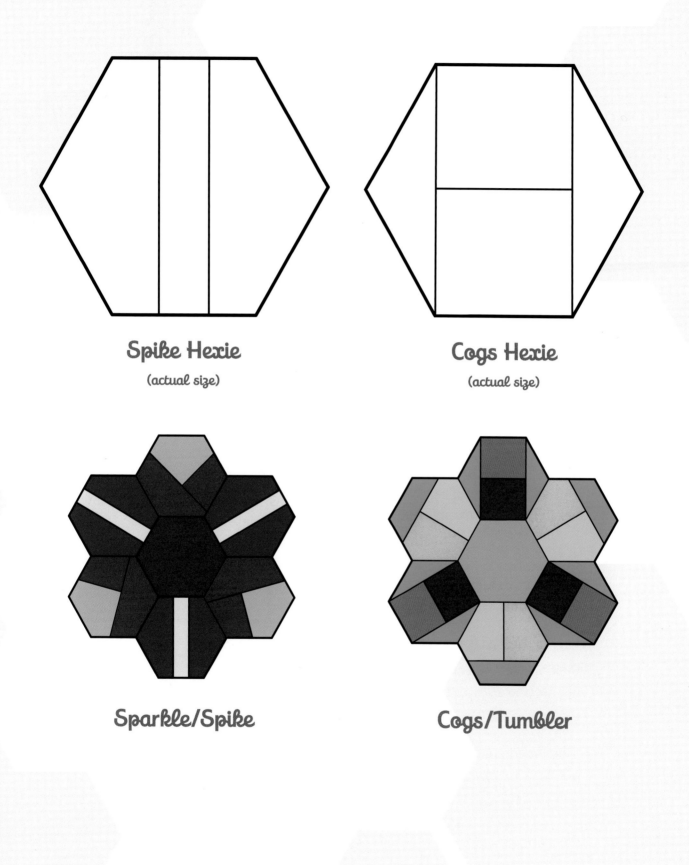

Spike Hexie

(actual size)

Cogs Hexie

(actual size)

Sparkle/Spike

Cogs/Tumbler

Sparkle

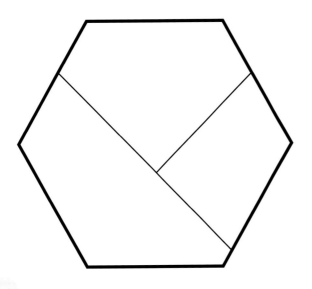

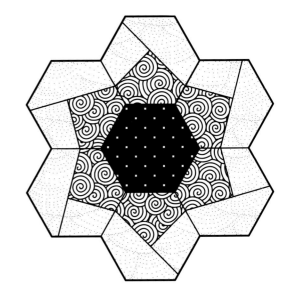

Be sure to read about *General Supplies, English Paper Piecing Instructions, and Pieced Hexie Basting Instructions* before you start.

These instructions are for piecing 6 – 3 ½" squares for each Sparkle rosette. The center hexagon is a solid fabric – no piecing instructions are needed, just use a 3 ½" square.

Important - Trim pieced seams to ⅛" after each one is sewn. This will reduce bulk for basting!

Material Needed for 1 Square

- ✪ Fabric A: 2 ¼" square
- ✪ Fabric B: 1 ¾" x 2 ¼"
- ✪ Fabric C: 1 ¾" x 3 ½"

Fabric Preparation

- ✪ Sew A to B lengthwise.
- ✪ Sew C across B/A unit. Make sure B/A orientation is the same for each square ... A is on the right

— OR —

Material Needed for 6 Squares

- ✪ Fabric A: 2 ¼" x 14 ½"
- ✪ Fabric B: 1 ¾" x 14 ½"
- ✪ Fabric C: (6) 1 ¾" x 3 ½"

Fabric Preparation

- ✪ Sew strips together lengthwise in A-B pattern.

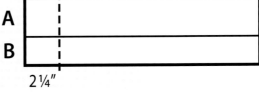

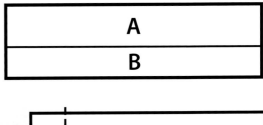

2¼"

⊛ Cut A-B into 2 ¼" segments and sew C across A/B unit length. Make sure the A/B orientation is the same for each square (A is on the right).

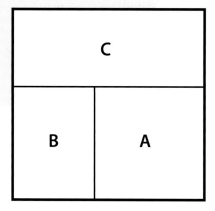

3 ½" Sparkle sewn square

Paper Preparation

Now baste the sewn square to the paper pattern. Perfect alignment is important, mark your paper hexagon with the alignment guides shown. Use a sharp pointed pencil or fine tip pen to mark lines. To mark accurately, angle your marking instrument tip into the groove of the ruler and paper.

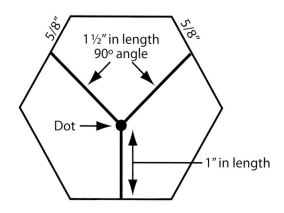

Sparkle Alignment Guides

⊛ Draw a very light line dividing hexagon in half from one edge to the other.

⊛ Mark a dot 1" from one edge

Using the **dot** as a guide, place ruler corner on the dot and line up 45° line on drawn line on

hexagon. Outside edges of ruler should each measure 1 ½" from the **dot** to the hexagon edge. Draw the outside edges.

Assembly

⊛ Place the sewn square with the seam side facing up.

⊛ Place the marked hexagon on top of sewn square with markings facing up. Put a pin thru the **dot** on hexagon perpendicular. Next put the point of the pin thru the intersection of the seams (where A-B-C meet).

⊛ Rotate the hexagon until the seam lines line up. Pin (second pin) once in the center, securing the sewn square to the paper. Remove the **dot** pin.

⊛ Trim away excess fabric, leaving a generous ¼" on each side for basting.

⊛ Baste the sewn square to the paper hexagon, using a running stitch. *Start your basting on an edge with a seam to secure.*

⊛ ***Do not*** *remove the pin until at least 3 sides are basted.*

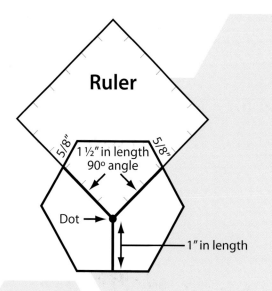

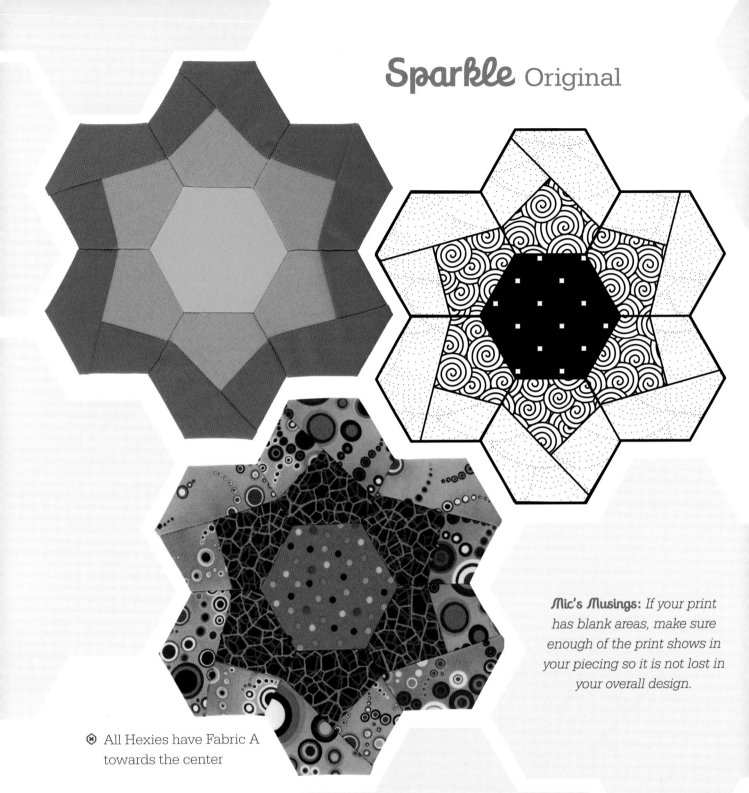

Sparkle Original

Mic's Musings: *If your print has blank areas, make sure enough of the print shows in your piecing so it is not lost in your overall design.*

✪ All Hexies have Fabric A towards the center

Sparkle Variation 1A

⊗ All Hexies have Fabric A towards the outer edge.

Mic's Musings: *Don't be afraid to place a dark dramatic fabric in the B/C areas for this design.*

Sparkle Variation 1B

Mic's Musings: *Stripes! Try actual line stripes or pattern that falls into stripes by design. Take the time to make sure all pieces flow in the same direction for a cohesive look.*

✪ Use a new fabric for piece C.

Sparkle Variation 2

⊗ The top 3 Hexies have fabric A at the lower edge.

⊗ The bottom 3 Hexies have fabric A at the upper edge.

Mic's Musings: A monochromatic print with a strong graphic pattern can add character to most any combination.

Sparkle Variation 3A

Mic's Musings: A dark fabric in the A sections gives this design a three-dimensional feel. The design created by the B/C pieces appears to be a pansy face to me.

⊗ Every other Hexie has fabric A either towards the center or towards the outside edge.

Sparkle Variation 3B

✸ Use a new fabric for piece C.

Mic's Musings: Be sure to use totally different prints in fabrics B and C so they can stand out separately.

Sparkle Variation 4

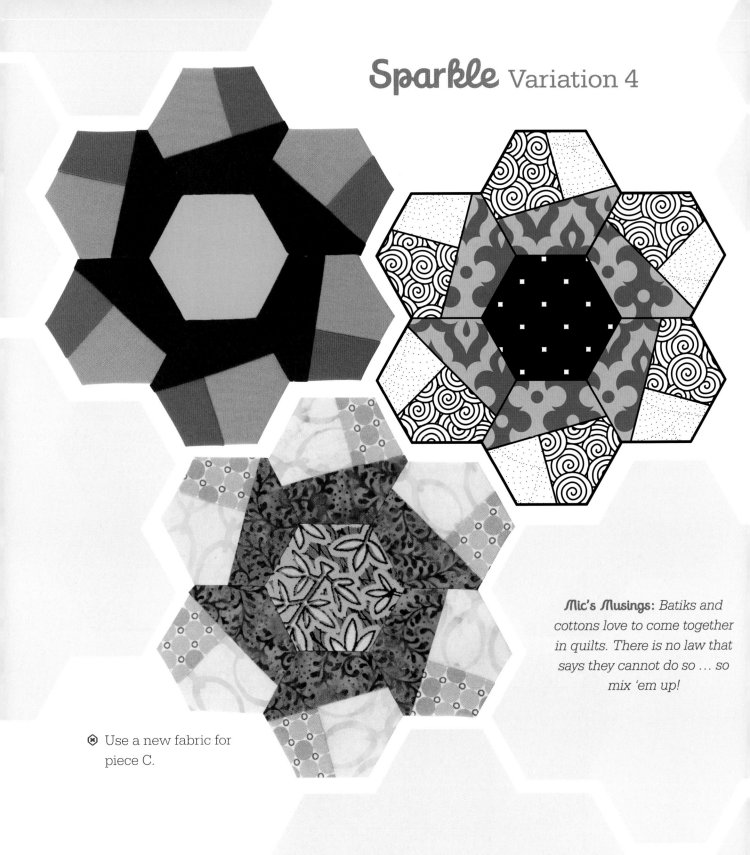

Mic's Musings: *Batiks and cottons love to come together in quilts. There is no law that says they cannot do so … so mix 'em up!*

⊗ Use a new fabric for piece C.

Sparkle Variation 5

⊛ Use a new fabric for piece C.

Mic's Musings: *High contrast in either fabric B or C is the way to go with this design.*

Sparkle Variation 6

Mic's Musings: *Don't be afraid to use a fabric that doesn't match the others in color but does work in style. It usually works out to be quite interesting.*

⊗ Use a new fabric for piece C.

What happens if you accidentally (or on purpose) turn the B/A section before sewing on piece C so that the orientation is A/B?

❋ Here is the outcome to the variations that use a third fabric for C.

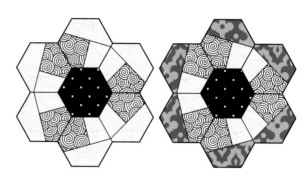

What if you took

❋ 3 Pieced Hexies - original orientation

❋ and 3 Pieced Hexies – reverse orientation

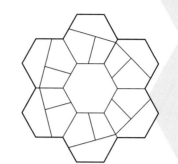

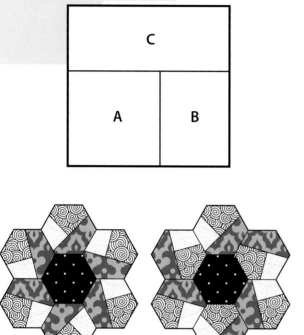

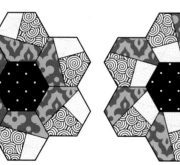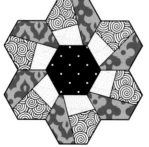

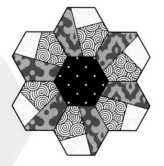

Sparkle 1/2 Reverse Combo Variation 2

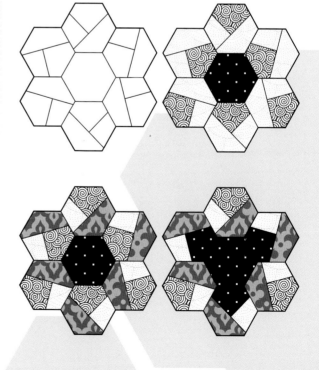

Tumbler

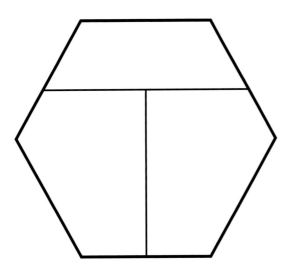

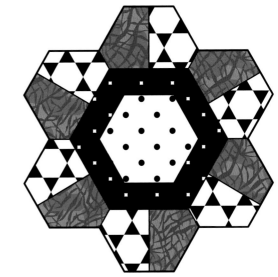

Be sure to read about General Supplies, English Paper Piecing Instructions, and Pieced Hexie Basting Instructions before you start.

These instructions are for piecing 6 – 3 ½" squares for each Tumbler rosette. The center hexagon is a solid fabric – no piecing instructions are needed, just use a 3 ½" square.

Important - Trim pieced seams to ⅛" after each one is sewn. This will reduce bulk for basting!

Material Needed for 1 Square

- ✪ Fabric A: 2" x 2 ½"
- ✪ Fabric B: 2" x 2 ½"
- ✪ Fabric C: 1 ½" x 3 ½"

Fabric Preparation

- ✪ Sew A to B along 2 ½" edges.
- ✪ Sew C across A/B unit. Make sure A/B orientation is the same for each square (A is on the left).

— **OR** —

Material Needed for 6 Squares

- ✪ Fabric A: 2" x 16"
- ✪ Fabric B: 2" x 16"
- ✪ Fabric C: (6) 1 ½" x 3 ½"

Fabric Preparation

- ✪ Sew strips together lengthwise in A-B pattern.

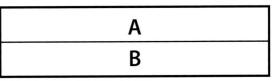

- ✪ Cut A-B into 2 ½" segments.

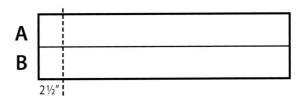

- ✪ Sew C to A/B unit.
- ✪ Make sure A/B orientation is the same for each square.
- ✪ **Note:** A is on the left.

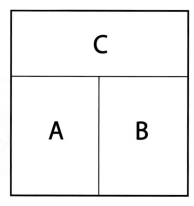

3 ½" Tumbler sewn square

Paper Preparation

Now baste the sewn square to the paper pattern. Perfect alignment is important, mark your paper hexagon with the alignment guides shown. Use a sharp pointed pencil or fine tip pen to mark lines. To mark accurately, angle your marking instrument tip into the groove of the ruler and paper.

Tumbler Alignment Guides

⊛ Measure ¾" from one edge and draw a line horizontally across hexagon.

⊛ Draw a line perpendicular from previously drawn line, dividing the larger space of divided hexagon in half.

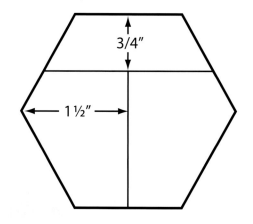

Assembly

⊛ Place the sewn square with the seam side facing up.

⊛ Place the marked paper pattern on top of the sewn square with markings facing up.

⊛ Line up the sewn seams and paper marks. Carefully pin once in the center, securing the sewn square to the paper.

⊛ Trim away excess fabric, leaving a generous ¼" on each side for basting.

⊛ Baste the sewn square to the paper hexagon, using a running stitch. *Start your basting on an edge with a seam to secure.*

⊛ **Do not** remove the pin until at least 3 sides are basted.

Tumbler Original

Mic's Musings: A solid-reading fabric in piece C will frame and show off your center choice.

48

Tumbler Variation 1

✪ Rotate Hexies once to the left.

Mic's Musings: Using a fabric that is different in color than the rest of the palette will spotlight that part of the design.

Mic's Musings: *Use a solid or a solid looking fabric and a dense print in the A/B positions. The contrast between them will give the illusion of dimension.*

- ⊛ Rotate Hexies twice to the left.
- ⊛ Fabric C will now be on the outer edge.

Tumbler Variation 3

⊗ For this variation, make half your pieced squares with fabric A on the left and half with fabric A on the right. This is done by simply turning half the squares before sewing on fabric C.

Mic's Musings: Place a print in the center triangle positions. Use high contrast/solid reading fabrics in all other positions to make this design sing.

Tumbler Variation 4

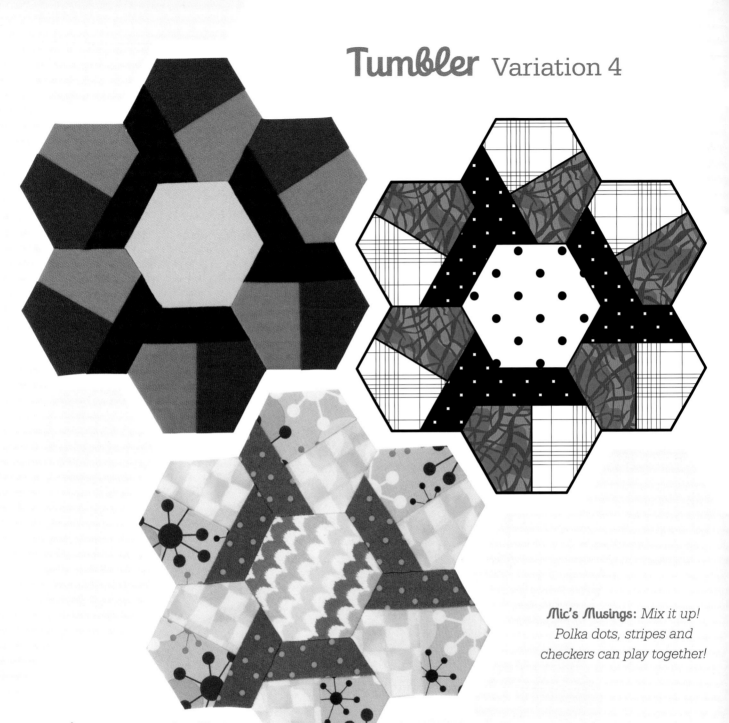

✹ Twist every other Hexie
from the original pattern
for a very unique look.

Mic's Musings: Mix it up!
Polka dots, stripes and
checkers can play together!

Tumbler Variation 5A

✸ Twist every other Hexie from the original pattern for a very unique look.

Mic's Musings: Colors don't have to match when repeating them (purple & blue in sample). Sometimes close enough is better than exact.

Tumbler Variation 5B

Mic's Musings: When using
2 prints next to each other,
make sure the scale of print is
different or the overall design
gets lost.

⊛ For this variation, make
half your pieced squares
with fabric A on the left
and half with fabric A
on the right. Simply turn
half the squares before
sewing on fabric C.

Tumbler Variation 6A

⊛ Twist every other Hexie from the
original pattern for a very unique
look.

*Mic's Musings: Plaid is so
misunderstood – try it. You'll
like it!*

Tumbler Variation 6B

Mic's Musings: The darker fabric doesn't always have to be toward the center in this design. Try putting it on the outer edge pieces.

⊗ For this variation, make half your pieced squares with fabric A on the left and half with fabric A on the right. Simply turn half the squares before sewing on fabric C.

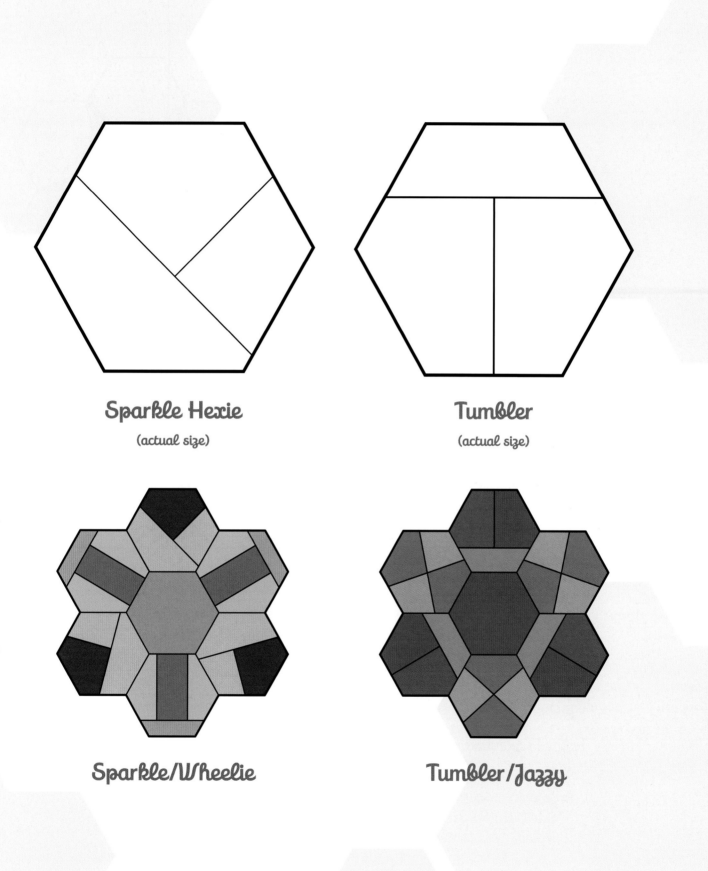

Sparkle Hexie

(actual size)

Tumbler

(actual size)

Sparkle/Wheelie

Tumbler/Jazzy

Jacks

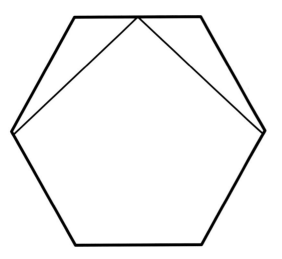

Be sure to read about *General Supplies, English Paper Piecing Instructions,* and *Pieced Hexie Basting Instructions* before you start.

These instructions are for piecing 6 – 3 ½" squares for each Jacks rosette. The center hexagon is a solid fabric – no piecing instructions are needed, just use a 3 ½" square.

Important - Trim pieced seams to ⅛" after each one is sewn. This will reduce bulk for basting!

Material Needed for 1 Square

- ✪ Fabric A: 3" square
- ✪ Fabric B: 1" x 3"
- ✪ Fabric C: 1" x 3 ½"

Fabric Preparation

- ✪ Sew A to B lengthwise.
- ✪ Sew C across the B/A unit. Make sure the B/A orientation is the same for each square - A is on the bottom.

— OR —

Material Needed for 6 Squares

- ✪ Fabric A: 3" x 19"
- ✪ Fabric B: 1" x 19"
- ✪ Fabric C: (6) 1" x 3 ½"

Fabric Preparation

- ✪ Sew the strips together lengthwise in A-B pattern.

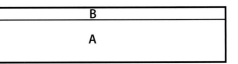

- ✪ Cut A-B into 3" segments and sew C across the A/B unit length. Make sure the A/B orientation is the same for each square (A is on the bottom).

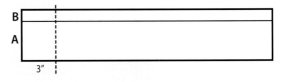

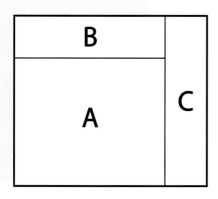

3 ½" Jacks sewn square

Paper Preparation

Now baste the sewn square to the paper pattern. Perfect alignment is important, mark your paper hexagon with the alignment guides shown. Use a sharp pointed pencil or fine tip pen to mark lines. To mark accurately, angle your marking instrument tip into the groove of the ruler and paper.

Jacks Alignment Guides

- ⊛ Mark a dot at the midpoint on one edge
- ⊛ Mark a dot ⅛" from one edge of corner(s) - that is 2 corner points to the left and 2 corner points to the right of the midpoint mark.
- ⊛ Using the dots as a guide, draw a line from midpoint to each ⅛" mark.

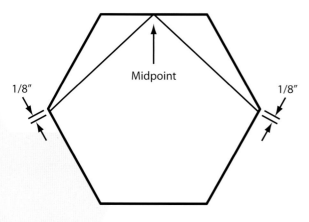

Assembly

- ⊛ Place the sewn square with the seam side facing up.
- ⊛ Place the marked paper pattern on top of the sewn square with markings facing up.
- ⊛ Line up the sewn seams and paper marks. Carefully pin once in the center, securing the sewn square to the paper.
- ⊛ Trim away excess fabric, leaving a generous ¼" on each side for basting.
- ⊛ Baste the sewn square to the paper hexagon, using a running stitch. *Start your basting on an edge with a seam to secure.*
- ⊛ ***Do not*** *remove the pin until at least 3 sides are basted.*

Jacks Original

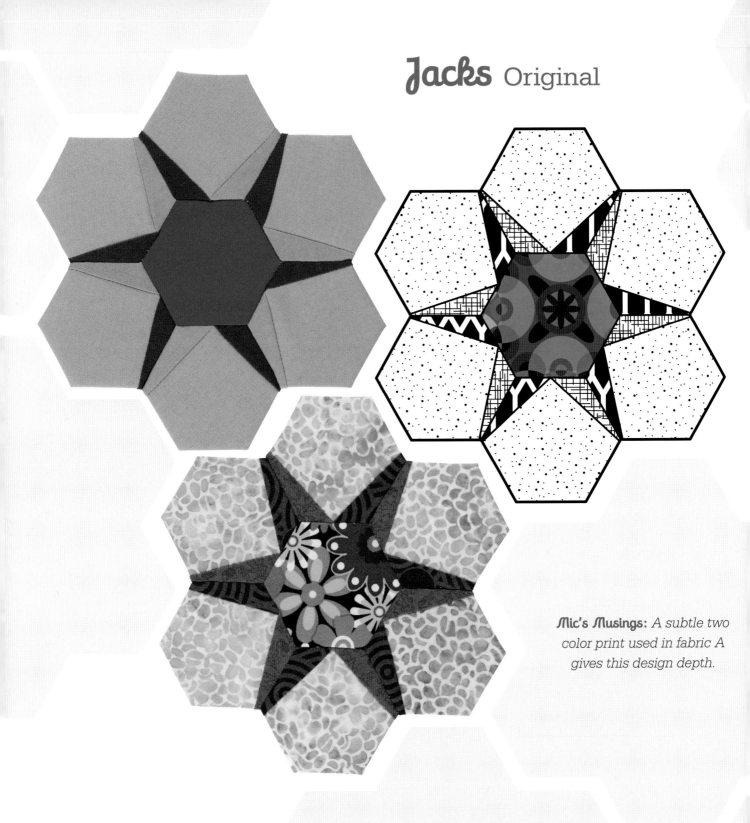

Mic's Musings: *A subtle two color print used in fabric A gives this design depth.*

Jacks Variation 1

✪ Rotate Hexies twice to the right.

Mic's Musings: Place black in the center and then repeat it in the C section – it makes those thin strips bolder.

Jacks Variation 2

⊗ From the original design,
flip every other Hexie
outward.

Mic's Musings:
*Monochromatic prints in the
B/C strips push the purple
print back and the dark center
forward in this design.*

Jacks Variation 3

✪ These Hexies have B/C fabrics on the outer edge.

Mic's Musings: Civil war prints sing a little louder when odd color combinations are paired.

Jacks Variation 4

Mic's Musings: I make no excuses … I love pattern. Don't be afraid of it … just remember to love your tonals and solids too.

⊛ The top 3 Hexies have fabric A at the upper edge.

⊛ The bottom 3 Hexies have fabric A at the lower edge.

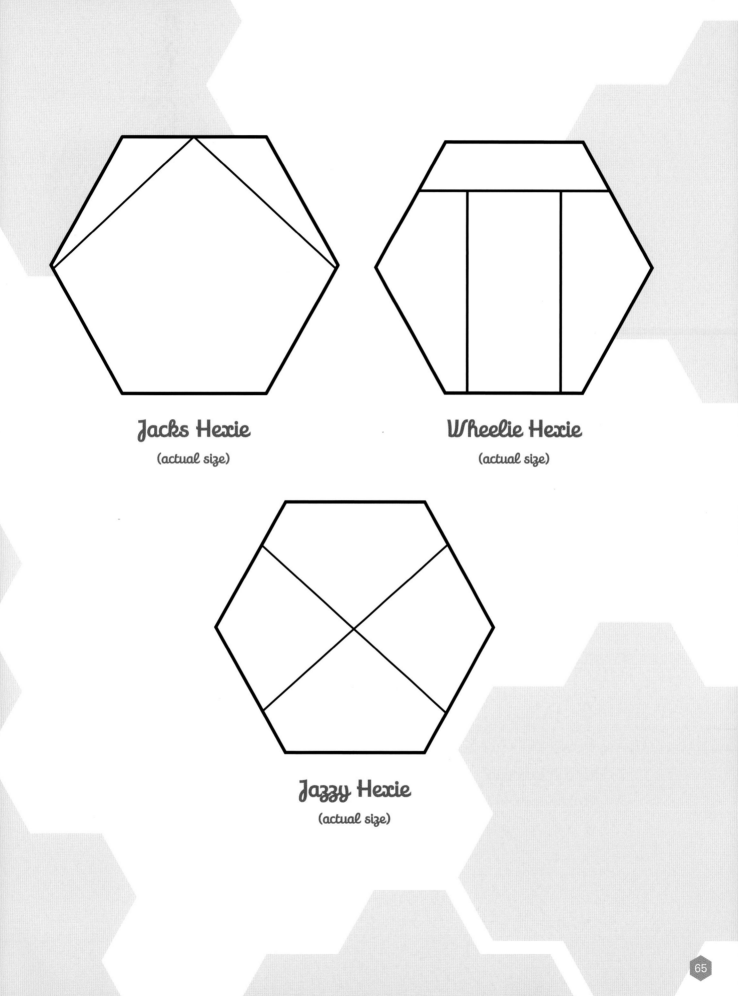

Jacks Hexie

(actual size)

Wheelie Hexie

(actual size)

Jazzy Hexie

(actual size)

Wheelie

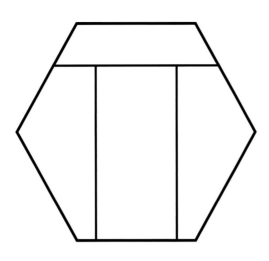

Be sure to read about General Supplies, English Paper Piecing Instructions, and Pieced Hexie Basting Instructions before you start.

These instructions are for piecing 6 – 3 ½" squares for each Wheelie rosette. The center hexagon is a solid fabric – no piecing instructions are needed, just use a 3 ½" square.

Important - Trim pieced seams to ⅛" after each one is sewn. This will reduce bulk for basting!

Material Needed for 1 Square

- ✪ Fabric A: 1 ½" x 2 ¾"
- ✪ Fabric B: (2) 1 ½" x 2 ¾"
- ✪ Fabric C: 1 ¼" x 3 ½"

Fabric Preparation

- ✪ Sew one B to A lengthwise on each side
- ✪ Sew C across B/A/B unit

— OR —

Material Needed for 6 Squares

- ✪ Fabric A: 1 ½" x 17 ½"
- ✪ Fabric B: (2) 1 ½" x 17 ½"
- ✪ Fabric C: (6) 1 ¼" x 3 ½"

Fabric Preparation

- ✪ Sew strips together lengthwise in B-A-B pattern.

B
A
B

- ✪ Cut B-A into 2 ¾" segments and sew C across the B/A/B unit length.

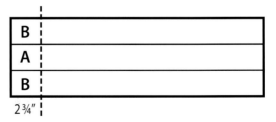

B
A
B

2 ¾"

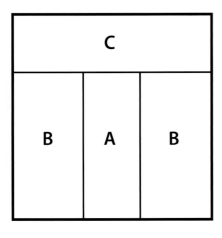

3 ½" Wheelie sewn square

Paper Preparation

Now baste the sewn square to the paper pattern. Perfect alignment is important, mark your paper hexagon with the alignment guides shown. Use a sharp pointed pencil or fine tip pen to mark lines. To mark accurately, angle your marking instrument tip into the groove of the ruler and paper.

Wheelie Alignment Guide

- ✹ Draw a line ½" from one edge - this is now considered the **top**.

- ✹ Using corner of **top** edge, measure ¼" and draw a line.

- ✹ Repeat in reverse on other **top** edge corner. You should now have a segment 1" wide down the center.

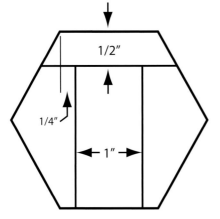

Assembly

- ✹ Place the sewn square with the seam side facing up.

- ✹ Place the marked paper pattern on top of the sewn square with markings facing up.

- ✹ Line up the sewn seams and paper marks. Carefully pin once in the center, securing the sewn square to the paper.

- ✹ Trim away excess fabric, leaving a generous ¼" on each side for basting.

- ✹ Baste the sewn square to the paper hexagon, using a running stitch. *Start your basting on an edge with a seam to secure.*

- ✹ **Do not** *remove the pin until at least 3 sides are basted.*

Wheelie Original A

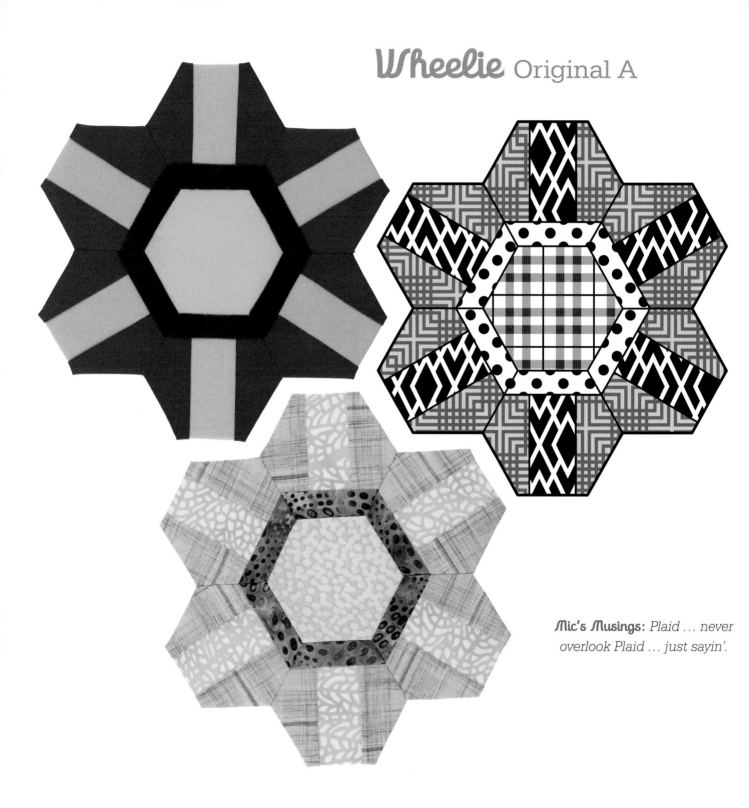

Mic's Musings: *Plaid … never overlook Plaid … just sayin'.*

Wheelie Original B

⊗ These Hexies have a fourth fabric added in place of either the left or right side B. Make all 6 Hexies alike.

Mic's Musings: *This design has 3 strips of nearly equal proportion lined up in a row. Two strips are dark and next to each other, the final strip is light - this gives you a paddlewheel look.*

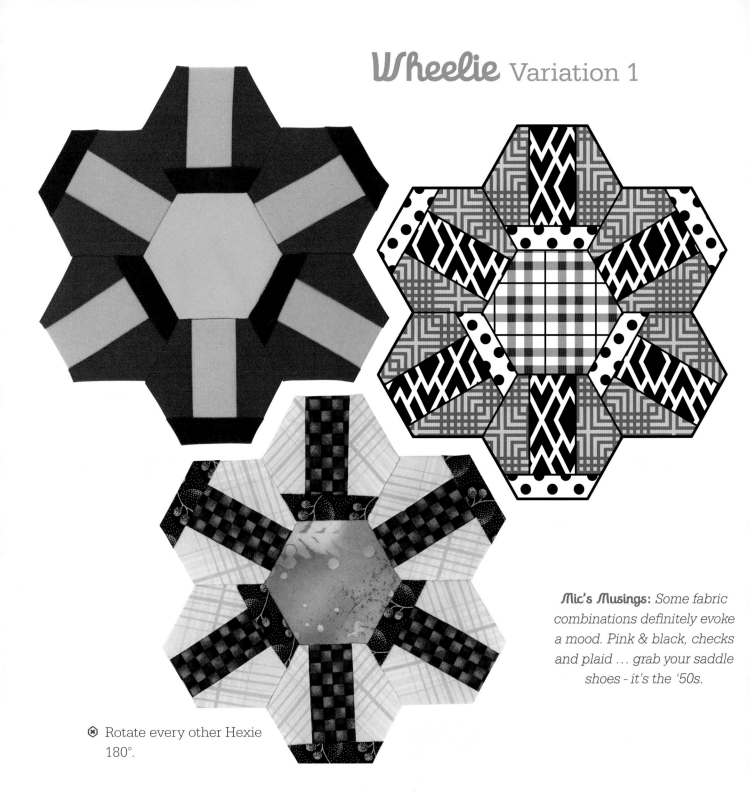

Mic's Musings: *Some fabric combinations definitely evoke a mood. Pink & black, checks and plaid … grab your saddle shoes - it's the '50s.*

✪ Rotate every other Hexie 180°.

Wheelie Variation 2A

✪ These Hexies have fabric C on the outer edge.

Mic's Musings: *I love Civil War prints. Try them once … they may not be your favorite but they are a whole new flavor.*

71

Wheelie Variation 2B

Mic's Musings: *The center print on the Hexies is actually cut off grain. Don't be afraid to twist your fabric once in awhile for a whole new look ... just be sure to sew up both sides as soon as possible to stabilize the edges.*

⊗ These Hexies have a fourth fabric added in place of either left or right side B. Make all 6 Hexies alike.

✪ Rotate Hexies twice to the right.

Mic's Musings: *The use of black (or any dark color) in the C location gives this design some spin.*

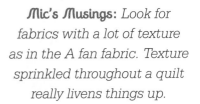

Mic's Musings: Look for fabrics with a lot of texture as in the A fan fabric. Texture sprinkled throughout a quilt really livens things up.

✪ These Hexies have a fourth fabric added in place of either left or right side B. Make all 6 Hexies alike.

Wheelie Variation 4A

⊗ Rotate Hexies once to the right.

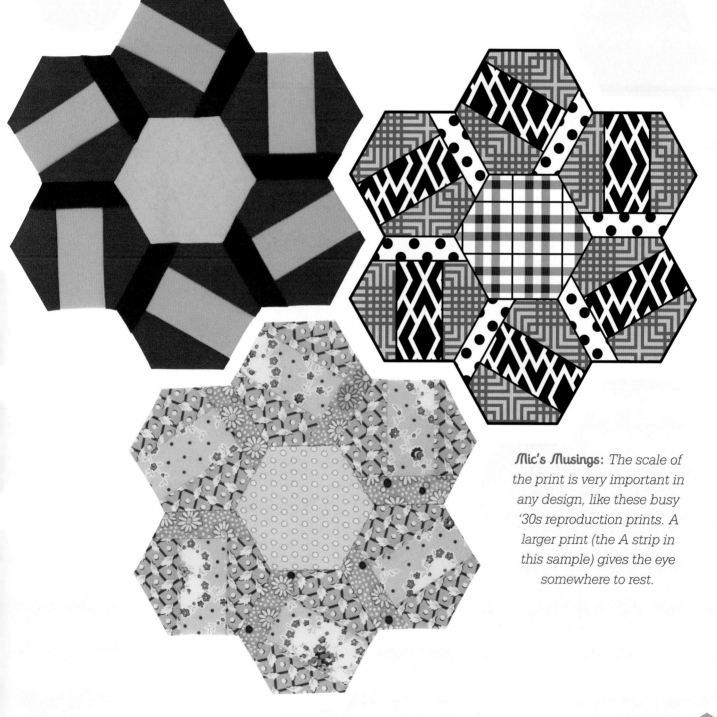

Mic's Musings: *The scale of the print is very important in any design, like these busy '30s reproduction prints. A larger print (the A strip in this sample) gives the eye somewhere to rest.*

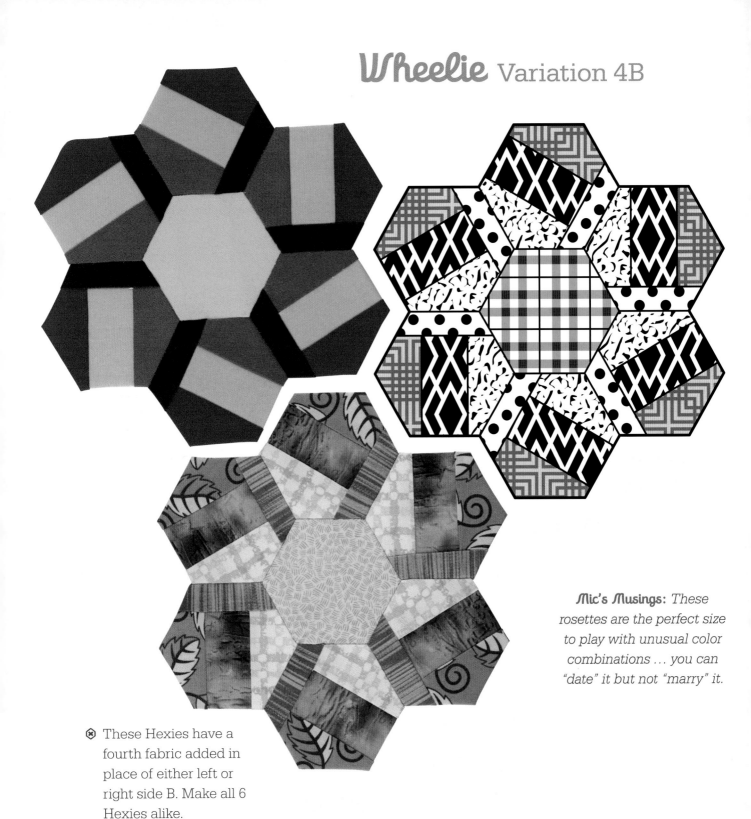

Mic's Musings: These rosettes are the perfect size to play with unusual color combinations ... you can "date" it but not "marry" it.

⬢ These Hexies have a fourth fabric added in place of either left or right side B. Make all 6 Hexies alike.

Wheelie Variation 5A

⊗ The fabric C edge meets in groups of two to form a double line of color/texture.

Mic's Musings: I suggest using a more solid reading fabric in the A spot to guarantee those bars in the design can be seen.

Mic's Musings: *Nothing matches in this sample but it all works because the fabrics are similar enough to hold hands. Using the soft tonal in the inner section of the design shows off the triangle pattern that is created.*

✸ These Hexies have a fourth fabric added in place of either left or right side B. Make all 6 Hexies alike.

Wheelie Variation 6

- ❋ The top 3 Hexies have fabric C at lower edge.
- ❋ The bottom 3 Hexies have fabric C at upper edge.

Mic's Musings: We all collect theme fabric. Pull it out and pair it up with some coordinating support fabrics so the "theme" doesn't become overwhelming.

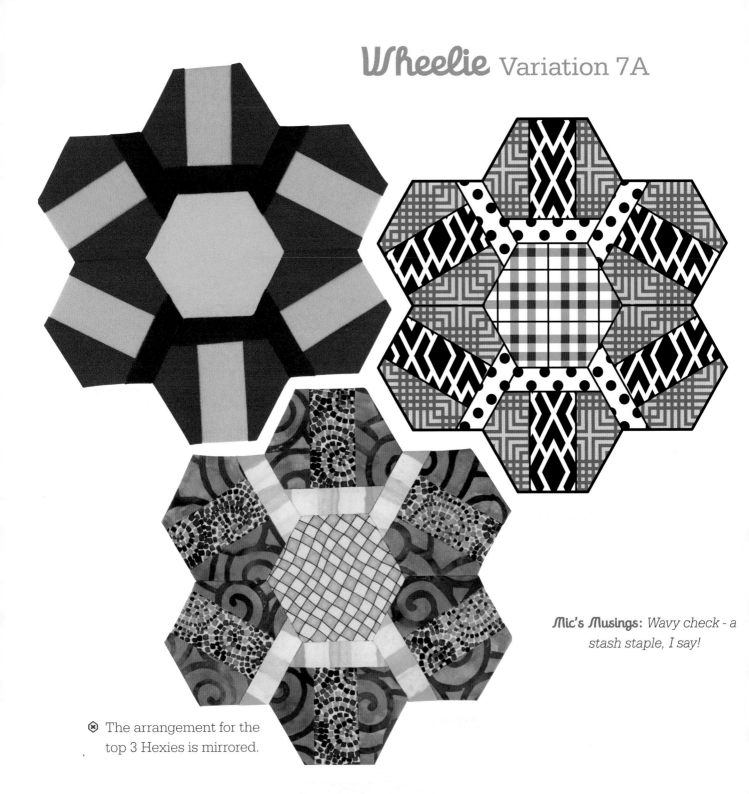

Mic's Musings: Wavy check - a stash staple, I say!

✳ The arrangement for the top 3 Hexies is mirrored.

Wheelie Variation 7B

- Four of these 6 Hexies have a fourth fabric added in place of either left or right side B.

- Two Hexies are the original B-A-B fabric format.

- Two Hexies are the B-A-D fabric format.

- Two Hexies are the D-A-B fabric format.

Mic's Musings: Putting a bold color/print in the inner section makes this design unique.

Wheelie Variation 8A

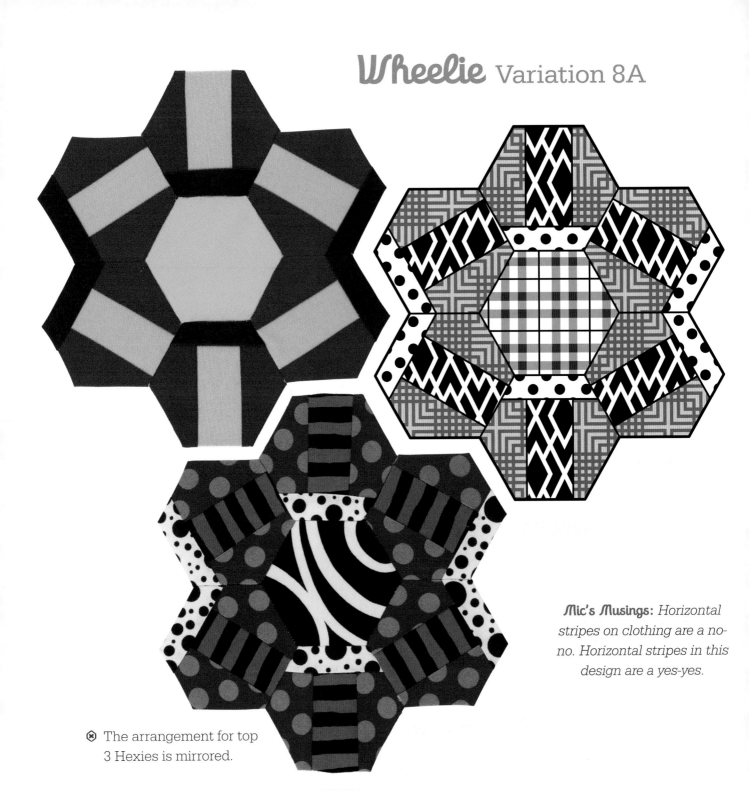

Mic's Musings: Horizontal stripes on clothing are a no-no. Horizontal stripes in this design are a yes-yes.

✸ The arrangement for top 3 Hexies is mirrored.

Wheelie Variation 8B

These Hexies have a fourth fabric added in place of either left or right side B (or both).

- ⊛ Two Hexies are the D-A-D fabric format.
- ⊛ Two Hexies are the B-A-D fabric format.
- ⊛ Two Hexies are the D-A-B fabric format.

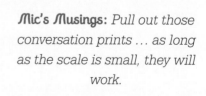

Mic's Musings: Pull out those conversation prints ... as long as the scale is small, they will work.

Jazzy

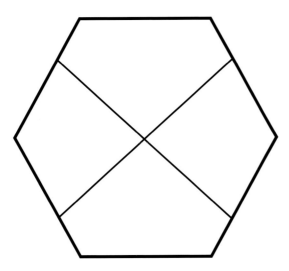

Be sure to read about General Supplies, English Paper Piecing Instructions, and Pieced Hexie Basting Instructions before you start.

These instructions are for piecing 6 – 3 ½" squares for each Jazzy rosette. The center hexagon is a solid fabric – no piecing instructions are needed, just use a 3 ½" square.

Important - Trim pieced seams to ⅛" after each one is sewn. This will reduce bulk for basting!

Material Needed for 1 Square

- ✺ Fabric A (2): 2" square
- ✺ Fabric B & C: 2" square

Fabric Preparation

- ✺ Sew A to B and A to C. Press toward A on both.
- ✺ Sew A/B to A/C in the style of a four-patch with the A's not touching except at the center.

— **OR** —

Material Needed for 6 Squares

- ✺ Fabric A(2 strips): 2" x 13"
- ✺ Fabric B & C: 2" x 13"

Fabric Preparation

- ✺ Sew strips together lengthwise making A/B and A/C. Press seams to A.

A
B

A
C

- ✺ Cut both strip sets into 2" segments.

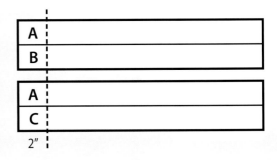

⊛ Sew A/B to A/C in the style of a four-patch with the A's not touching except at center.

3 ½" Jazzy sewn square

Paper Preparation

Now baste the sewn square to the paper pattern. Perfect alignment is important, mark your paper hexagon with the alignment guides shown. Use a sharp pointed pencil or fine tip pen to mark lines. To mark accurately, angle your marking instrument tip into the groove of the ruler and paper.

Jazzy Alignment Guide

⊛ Measure a scant 1 ⅛" from center corners (both left and right) and mark.

⊛ Draw intersecting lines from opposite marks. Lines will cross in the center.

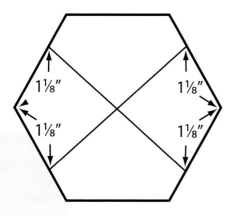

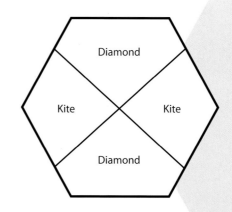

⊛ Look at the 4 segments on this Hexie.

⊛ Two will be referred to as **Diamonds** and the other two as **Kites**.

Assembly

⊛ Place the sewn square with the seam side facing up.

⊛ Place the marked paper pattern on top of the sewn square with markings facing up.

⊛ Line up the sewn seams and paper marks. Carefully pin once in the center, securing the sewn square to the paper.

⊛ Trim away excess fabric, leaving a generous ¼" on each side for basting.

⊛ Baste the sewn square to the paper hexagon, using a running stitch. *Start your basting on an edge with a seam to secure.*

⊛ **Do not** *remove the pin until at least 3 sides are basted.*

Mic's Musings: *Loud fabrics in color and print can be calmed by using neutrals (taupe, cream, gray, white, black) in your combination.*

⊛ All the same Diamonds are toward the center.

Jazzy Original B

⊗ Flip every other Hexie, placing opposite Diamonds toward the edge.

Mic's Musings: Same scale prints in different colors can work together if there is enough contrast.

Jazzy Original C

Mic's Musings: The stripes in this design accentuate the swirl.

✪ Switch fabrics so B/C-Diamonds will be the same and A-Kites are split into 2 choices.

Jazzy Variation 1

⊛ Twist Hexies so the C-Diamonds
pair up 3 times with their long
edges touching.

*Mic's Musings: Don't be
afraid of those high pattern
geometric prints.*

Jazzy Variation 2

Mic's Musings: *Brown likes to be the focus once in a while. It is often overlooked.*

⊗ Working in groups of 2, twist the left Hexie once clockwise and the right Hexie counter clockwise. Repeat with the remaining 4 Hexies.

Jazzy Variation 3

- Starting at the top, twist every other Hexie once counterclockwise. Diamonds are on an angle from the center. Flip the remaining Hexies 180°, changing the Diamond fabric that touches the center.

Mic's Musings: *If a fabric has multiple colors in it, use it in the areas of greatest exposure so all colors can be seen.*

Jazzy Variation 4

Mic's Musings:
Monochromatic fabric with texture is always an asset.

- ✪ The top 3 Hexies have fabric B (or C) at lower edge.
- ✪ The bottom 3 Hexies have fabric B (or C) at upper edge.

Jazzy Variation 5

⊛ Rotate the upper left Hexie one twist counter clockwise.

⊛ Rotate the upper right Hexie one twist clockwise.

⊛ Repeat for the lower Hexies using opposite directional movement for right and left.

⊛ Flip the upper center Hexies (top and bottom) 180°.

Mic's Musings: You can use 2 fabrics with dots ... just make sure the scale of print is different to make it work.

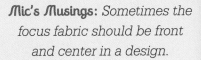

Mic's Musings: Sometimes the focus fabric should be front and center in a design.

⊛ Piece 2 Hexies (center Hexies - top and bottom) following the original fabric orientation (page 86).

⊛ Piece 4 Hexies following Jazzy Original C (page 88). Place these 4 Hexies on the upper and lower outer edges.

Resource Guide

APQS – longarm machines & **GEORGE!** (my machine for quilting)
www.apqs.com

Bernina of America –sewing machine, of course
www.berninausa.com

Clover – needle threader
www.clover-usa.com

Colonial Needle Company – needles and Prescenia Thread
www.colonialneedle.com

Electric Quilt – Boutique Collection of ALL designs in Pieced Hexies for easy designing
www.electricquilt.com

Ken's Handmade Wooden – seam ripper
www.quiltnbee.biz (look under notions-other)

Paper Pieces – English paper piecing supplies
www.paperpieces.com

Thread – silk thread
ylicorp.com

Note: Websites can change daily. These two had hexagon images available for free download as we prepared this book. I suggest you look at them or google "hexagon template" to find what is available at the time of your search.

Websites with hexagon images:

0 to 5
www.0to5.com.au/templates/hexagon.htm.

Wikimedia Commons
www.commons.wikimedia.org/wiki/File:Regular_hexagon.svg

A blank Hexie is just a wanna-be Pieced Hexie
- Mickey Depre